CHICAGO
THE CITY AT A GLANCE

Lake Point Tower
Still a desirable ad...
Point has
See p081

John Hanc...
SOM's glow...
signposts the
See p080

Aqua Tower
An exemplar of sustainable architecture, its
undulating balconies are stunning close up.
See p073

Aon Center
This strict, severe but actually quite endearing
tower looms to the north of Millennium Park.
See p013

Trump Tower
Considering its lineage, the 2009 leviathan is
rather accomplished. Architect Adrian Smith's
423m design echoes his Burj Khalifa in Dubai.
401 N Wabash Avenue

Marina City
Bertrand Goldberg's cylinders are charming
concrete remnants of 1960s idealism.
See p015

Chicago Board of Trade
The undoubted jewel of the city's commerce
corridor is this 1930 art deco masterpiece.
141 W Jackson Boulevard

Willis Tower
Overtaken as the States' tallest building by
One World Trade Center in NYC, it nonetheless
remains a supremely elegant mega-structure.
See p012

INTRODUCTION

THE CHANGING FACE OF THE URBAN SCENE

Despite the lure of its suburbs, which continue to entice urbanites from the centre, Chicago proper remains firmly in the ascendancy. The 'city of broad shoulders', long associated with political cynicism, organised crime, blues and jazz (perhaps the truest of US artforms) and architecture at its most daring and adventurous, is once again a confident, hopeful place, mainly due to the ingenuity of both its entrepreneurs and creative community. This is the most American of America's metropolises, and it has paid for it. A one-time rival to New York, it suffered in comparison to the global player, then felt the pain as Los Angeles' glitz eclipsed its meat and smoke. Now, interesting in part simply because it is *not* LA or NYC, Chicago has reinvented itself. The hog butcher to the world has become one of the cleanest and most attractive destinations in the States.

It is incontrovertible that The Loop is an unusual proposition. Look skywards and you will see the iconography of civic ambition, fronted by Millennium Park (see p067), a public space of radical intention. Yet down on the street there are shabby storefronts and panhandlers, although a residential boom is imminent. Elsewhere, regeneration has already run its course in Bucktown and Wicker Park, allowing 'hoods such as Pilsen, Logan Square and Avondale, which are filling up with shops, bars and restaurants, to come into their own. Chicago is still working out how it gets from what it was to what it wants to be, and that is what makes it truly invigorating.

ESSENTIAL INFO

FACTS, FIGURES AND USEFUL ADDRESSES

TOURIST OFFICE
Choose Chicago
77 E Randolph Street
www.choosechicago.com

TRANSPORT
Airport transfer to city centre
Blue Line trains depart regularly, 24 hours
a day. The journey takes about 40 minutes
www.transitchicago.com/airports
Car hire
Avis
214 N Clark Street
T 312 782 6825
www.avis.com
Taxis
Chicago Carriage Cab Co
T 312 326 2221
Trains
Chicago Transit Authority
T 312 836 7000
www.transitchicago.com
Red and Blue Lines operate a 24-hour
service; all the other routes run from
approximately 5am to 1.30am
Travel card
A three-day CTA pass costs around $20

EMERGENCY SERVICES
Emergencies
T 911
24-hour pharmacy
Walgreens
641 N Clark Street
T 312 587 1416

CONSULATE-GENERAL
British Consulate-General
Suite 2200
625 N Michigan Avenue
T 312 970 3800
www.gov.uk/government/world/usa

POSTAL SERVICES
Post office
540 N Dearborn Street
T 312 644 3919
Shipping
UPS
T 312 917 1705

BOOKS
Chicago Makes Modern edited by
Mary Jane Jacob and Jacquelynn Baas
(University of Chicago Press)
Theaster Gates with texts by Carol
Becker, Lisa Lee and Achim Borchardt-
Hume (Phaidon)
The Man with the Golden Arm
by Nelson Algren (Seven Stories Press)

WEBSITES
Architecture
www.architecture.org
Newspaper
www.chicagoreader.com

EVENTS
Chicago Architecture Biennial
www.chicagoarchitecturebiennial.org
Expo Chicago
www.expochicago.com

COST OF LIVING
**Taxi from O'Hare International
Airport to city centre**
$60
Cappuccino
$4
Packet of cigarettes
$12
Daily newspaper
$2
Bottle of champagne
$60

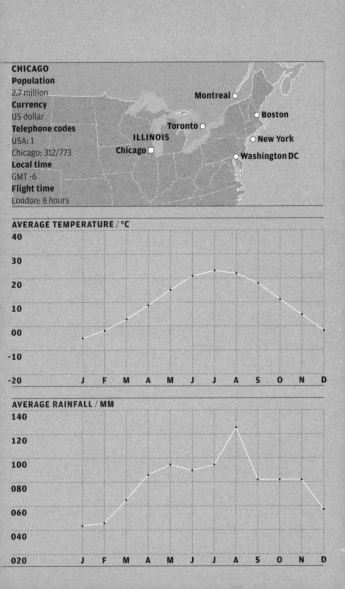

CHICAGO
Population
2.7 million
Currency
US dollar
Telephone codes
USA: 1
Chicago: 312/773
Local time
GMT -6
Flight time
London: 8 hours

ILLINOIS

Montreal
Toronto
Boston
New York
Washington DC
Chicago

AVERAGE TEMPERATURE / °C

| | | | | | | | | | | | |
|40|
|30|
|20|
|10|
|00|
|-10|
|-20| J | F | M | A | M | J | J | A | S | O | N | D |

AVERAGE RAINFALL / MM

| | | | | | | | | | | | |
|140|
|120|
|100|
|080|
|060|
|040|
|020| J | F | M | A | M | J | J | A | S | O | N | D |

NEIGHBOURHOODS

THE AREAS YOU NEED TO KNOW AND WHY

To help you navigate the city, we've chosen the most interesting districts (see below and the map inside the back cover) and colour-coded our featured venues, according to their location; those venues that are outside these areas are not coloured.

THE LOOP

The dead centre of the city is an architects' playground – innumerable skyscrapers cluster in-between Millennium Park (see p067) to the east and the Chicago River and the financial district to the west. The L train clatters overhead, providing the best viewing platform, while drab chain stores proliferate at ground level.

LINCOLN PARK

For the past 30 years, this comfortable residential zone, named after Chicago's largest park, has been inhabited by the young monied folk. W Armitage Avenue has a concentration of once-cool retail and eating opportunities, now put in the shade by Wicker Park and the West Loop.

SOUTH LOOP

After decades in the doldrums, the South Loop has gentrified, via loft conversions and destination restaurants like Acadia (1639 S Wabash Avenue, T 312 360 9500). The imposing warehouses that formed the backdrop to Al Capone's misdemeanours are still here, which just adds to the charm.

NEAR NORTH

Bisected by the Magnificent Mile, a stretch of Michigan Avenue packed with upmarket shops and luxury hotels, this is invariably where visitors to the city first land; some of its most distinctive landmarks are here (see p080). River North is the location of a robust community of galleries (see p056).

WEST LOOP

The meatpacking district (which is centred on Fulton Market) and its environs make up the West Loop. Its former warehouses are now colonised by loft dwellers, smart galleries like Kavi Gupta (see p026) and Andrew Rafacz (see p066), and fashionable dining spots, such as Duck Duck Goat (see p034) and Roister (see p032).

GOLD COAST

Named after the colour of the money in its residents' coffers, this is where you'll come across some of Chicago's most extravagant mansions, near Astor Street, and a clutch of high-end shops and eateries, including Alinea (see p044). Oak Street Beach offers opportunities for some lakeside R&R.

ANDERSONVILLE/LAKE VIEW

North Side's Andersonville has emerged as a hotbed for design retail (see p089). To the south, the primarily residential Lake View absorbs smaller 'hoods like Wrigleyville, home to one of the country's best-loved ballparks Wrigley Field, and Boystown, the hub of Chicago's gay scene.

WICKER PARK/LOGAN SQUARE

Favoured by art and music types, as well as the stroller crowd, Wicker Park is laidback and mainly low-rise, full of hip boutiques and restaurants, and the chic Robey hotel (see p018). The trendsetters are in Logan Square, a hot zone for great dining rooms, bars and cafés, including Lula (see p054).

LANDMARKS
THE SHAPE OF THE CITY SKYLINE

No other modern city has attempted to create as many landmark structures as Chicago. A collective and corporate will – as well as a certain civic cheerfulness – has seen America's then second, now third, city put up the first skyscrapers and spend the next century sending them ever higher while refining and redefining the form.

It makes for a unique and navigable landscape, less dense than New York's but unmatched in its historical and stylistic stretch. Two dark giants, the Willis Tower (see p012) and John Hancock Center (see p080), practically bookend downtown. At street level, public art is prevalent; most key buildings have an accompanying sculptural statement, by the likes of Calder, Chagall or Picasso. No surprise, then, that one of the more recent landmarks is a cluster of truly public artwork. In Millennium Park (see p067), Frank Gehry's Jay Pritzker Pavilion, Jaume Plensa's *Crown Fountain* and Anish Kapoor's *Cloud Gate* have become instant icons.

Now attention is being paid to the waterfront with Studio Gang's boathouses (see p086) and its masterplan for the redevelopment of Northerly Island. And, if anything ever gets out of the ground at 400 N Lake Shore Drive (the site of two super-tall proposals by first Calatrava and then Gensler), it might just become the totem for Chicago re-establishing itself as a great American city. Perhaps, as Norman Mailer proclaimed 50 years ago, *the* great American city. *For full addresses, see Resources*.

Tribune Tower

In 1922, Colonel Robert McCormick, the publisher of the *Chicago Tribune*, launched a competition to design the company's HQ, heralding a new age in US architecture. The second-placed entry, by Eliel Saarinen, was a muscular tower with flourishes and setbacks that looked eerily like a truncated proto-Empire State Building (a design by Walter Gropius and Adolf Meyer seems an even more startling premonition of the Chicago yet to come). The winner was less avant-garde – an outsized Gothic fantasy from New York practice Raymond Hood and John Mead Howells. The high-rise is topped by an almost absurd abstraction of Rouen Cathedral, flying buttresses and all. Now that Chicago boasts more modernism than it knows what to do with, the Tribune's presence is a welcome grand extravagance.
435 N Michigan Avenue

150 North Riverside

Chicago hadn't had a new trophy building since 2010's Aqua Tower (see p073) until 150 North Riverside arrived seven years later. When seen from the river, Goettsch Partners' 54-storey skyscraper is, due to its gravity-defying appearance, rather awe-inducing. It appears to have pin-dropped into its plot, wedged between seven active Amtrak railway lines and the waterfront. To negotiate the tight site, and give space for parkland at ground level, it cantilevers from a central core, dramatically flaring out from a 14m-wide base. The facade is divided into volumes, so the structure appears as if it is a collection of separate towers, accentuating its slenderness. An assemblage of enormous water tanks in the upper floors prevents it from swaying.
150 N Riverside Plaza,
www.150northriverside.com

Willis Tower

Inaugurated in 1974, the 110-storey Willis Tower (formerly called Sears) held the title of the world's tallest building until 1998. The nine bundled skyscrapers of different heights, conceived by Bruce Graham and engineer Fazlur Khan of Skidmore, Owings & Merrill, are wonderfully debonair. The distinctive cluster design (Graham was allegedly inspired while considering the profile of cigarettes popping out of a pack) allows it to soar. At 442m high (and 527m right up to the tip), it may well have been overtaken by the Petronas Twin Towers in Kuala Lumpur (1998), followed by Taipei 101 (2004), the Shanghai World Finance Center (2008), Hong Kong's ICC Tower and Dubai's Burj Khalifa (both 2010), but in terms of sheer architectural bravado, it stands alone among the global giants. *223 S Wacker Drive, www.willistower.com*

Aon Center

First known as the Standard Oil Building (dubbed 'Big Stan'), this 346m skyscraper temporarily reigned as the city's highest after its completion in 1973 (a helicopter had indicated how tall it was going to be at the ground-breaking ceremony). It only had this honour for a matter of months before it was overtaken, and then some, by the Willis Tower (opposite), but its position and the gracefulness of Edward Durell Stone's design make it one of Chicago's most emblematic, if not best-loved, towers. The structure was clad in 43,000 marble panels, but when they started to come away in the 1980s, threatening to tumble some 300m, they were replaced with white granite at a cost of more than $60m. The sculptural accompaniment, in the plaza, is a set of metal wind rods by Harry Bertoia. *200 E Randolph Street*

Lake Shore Drive apartments

Mies van der Rohe's relocation from Nazi Germany to Chicago was fortuitous in so many ways. One stroke of luck was him meeting developer Herbert Greenwald. Despite Greenwald's youth – he was 31 when they first collaborated in 1946 – he was brave enough to back the architect's vision (although apparently less generous when it came to prompt payments). That vision found almost perfect expression in the four glass towers they put up between 1949 and 1955. The first two, at 860-880 Lake Shore Drive (above), were Mies' first to use glass-and-steel curtain walls with no interior load-bearing walls. The second pair, at No 900-910, are a slightly darker echo of the originals. Chicagoans took to the skyscrapers, and this new modern way of life, as if it were their birthright. *860-880 and 900-910 N Lake Shore Drive*

Marina City

An attempt to revitalise the then struggling city centre, the 1964 'corn cob' towers are unavoidable, and somehow manage to be as charming as 65 storeys of reinforced concrete can be. And even in a place so rich in superlative buildings, they are up there as totemic mascots (local sons, the band Wilco, put Marina City on the cover of their 2002 album *Yankee Hotel Foxtrot*). They were designed by Bertrand Goldberg, who had studied under Mies van der Rohe at the Bauhaus. After returning to the US in the 1930s, the architect later developed a very non-Miesian sense of playfulness and a distaste for right angles. In 1972, the unveiling of Mies' nearby IBM Building, now AMA Plaza and home to The Langham hotel (see p021), makes it clear just how much Goldberg had gone his merry way.
300 N State Street

HOTELS

WHERE TO STAY AND WHICH ROOMS TO BOOK

Chicago's hotel scene is highly evolved. There is an embarrassment of choice when it comes to deluxe suites, from The Peninsula (108 E Superior Street, T 312 337 2888), which holds a prime position on the Magnificent Mile and has a knockout swimming pool (see p025), to The Ritz-Carlton (160 E Pearson Street, T 312 266 1000) and the Four Seasons (120 E Delaware Place, T 312 280 8800). Other high-end alternatives are the Sofitel (20 E Chestnut Street, T 312 324 4000) and Park Hyatt (800 N Michigan Avenue, T 312 335 1234). In addition, refurbishments tend to be frequent, so what is tired one year may have a million-dollar makeover the next.

Despite this being a city at the forefront of modern architecture, it used to be that hotel interiors were relatively pedestrian. That is no longer the case, and many venues have plenty of added interest too. The Langham (see p021) is as sleek as its Mies van der Rohe building (see p015); while the InterContinental (505 N Michigan Avenue, T 312 944 4100) occupies a 1929 former sports club and has an original art deco pool. Boutique hotels have been growing in number. Where once The James (see p022) was almost alone in this niche, visitors can now choose between The Gray (opposite), The Robey (see p018), Chicago Athletic Association (see p020) and Soho House (113-125 N Green Street, T 312 521 8000), which has been stylishly wrought out of an historic 1907 warehouse. *For full addresses and room rates, see Resources.*

The Gray

Gracefully inserted into William Le Baron Jenney's former New York Life Insurance Building, an 1894 pile, The Gray is named after the original Georgia marble that still seems to glimmer. Design firm Beleco has retained the terracotta and brick facade, and the public spaces are comfortable and stylish, featuring a bevy of classic pieces, such as Bruno Mathsson's leather loungers and a shaggy, rather fabulous, armchair by Laura Kirar. The 293 rooms follow suit; our favourite is the King Spa Studio. The minibars are stocked with useful, playful items, such as a tie, lapel pin and pocket square. Head to rooftop Boleo (T 312 750 9007) for Peruvian small plates, and Vol 39 (T 312 604 9909) off the lobby (above) for fine cocktails, caviar and charcuterie. *122 W Monroe Street, T 877 771 7031, www.grayhotelchicago.com*

The Robey

Belgian architects Nicolas Schuybroek have carved out 69 rooms (Corner Suite, above) from the art deco Northwest Tower, designed by Perkins, Chatten & Hammond and finished in 1929. Its interiors by Marc Merckx have a cool industrial feel warmed up with hardwood floors, terrazzo tiling, marble tabletops, gun-metal paint, grey wool blankets and accents of oxide red. The sixth-floor Cabana Club has a pool located atop the adjoining sister property Robey Hall (T 872 315 3080), which is a hip, upscale hostel in the 1905 Hollander Fireproof Warehouse. The rooftop Up & Up lounge bar and terrace (opposite), tucked under the Jazz Age spire, is one of the real draws here – a honey-toned, sophisticated hangout strewn with minimalist furniture. *2018 W North Avenue, T 872 315 3050, www.therobey.com*

Chicago Athletic Association

Henry Ives Cobb's 1893 Venetian Gothic building served as a social club for a string of elite sports and business families who formed the Chicago Athletic Association. It was transformed into a 241-room hotel by native firm Hartshorne Plunkard, with interiors by Roman and Williams, that pays tribute to its storied past. Many features have been retained, from the facade to the stained-glass windows, marble staircases and a grand ballroom. Soak up the history in a Founders Suite (above), which have a litany of period details, be it a working fireplace, intricate woodwork, mosaic tiles or a wrought-iron bathtub. Do not miss Milk Room (T 312 792 3515), a tucked-away eight-seater bar (book ahead) that uses vintage spirits in its first-class cocktails. *12 S Michigan Avenue, T 312 940 3552, www.chicagoathletichotel.com*

The Langham

Occupying the first 13 floors of Mies van
der Rohe's landmark high-rise, completed
in 1972 after the architect's death in 1969,
the 316-room Langham is a seductive blend
of classic modernism and contemporary
luxury. Richmond International's interior
renovation and decor is pitch-perfect in its
chic colour palette and refined materials.
The first-floor lobby (above) was entrusted
to Mies' grandson, Chicago architect Dirk
Lohan, who custom-designed a desk based
on a Mies original in Farnsworth House
(see p102). Artistic embellishments include
a Jaume Plensa sculpture and painting by
Enoc Perez. The restaurant, Travelle (T 312
923 7705), is the work of David Rockwell.
Opt for one of the Classic River View Suites
and luxuriate in the setting, inside and out.
330 N Wabash Avenue, T 312 923 9988,
www.chicago.langhamhotels.com

The James

Setting out to bridge the gap between the boutique and the luxury categories, The James has accomplished this with some aplomb. It has a unique, unstuffy air and offers the kind of discreet service that you usually only encounter at the old-school end of the market. NYC architect Deborah Berke was responsible for the decor. It's a mix of earth tones, stone and warm timber punctuated with well-placed 20th-century design classics, which is another magnet for a style-savvy clientele. There are almost 300 rooms here (Penthouse Loft, above and opposite, replete with vintage Eames 'Lounge Chair'), each with platform beds and slate-tiled bathrooms. Downstairs, steak restaurant Primehouse (T 312 660 6000) remains popular, while the cocktails in the lavish bar lure those worn out from flexing their cards on the Magnificent Mile. *55 E Ontario Street, T 312 337 1000, www.jameshotels.com/chicago*

24 HOURS

SEE THE BEST OF THE CITY IN JUST ONE DAY

Few cities are as defined by their transport systems as Chicago is by the L, or elevated train. The first sections date to 1892, and today the network is slow, crowded and in need of serious investment. But it does allow you to glide two storeys high – a rocking, rickety ride – through the towers of The Loop and out into the various neighbourhoods, some hip and gentrified, others dilapidated.

Start in South Loop, taking in Printers Row, once the location of nearly 100 printing houses, like George C Nimmons' 1916 Franklin Building (720 S Dearborn Street). The streets are reminiscent of an early gangster movie, but now house the loft-living literati. Grab a coffee at Intelligentsia (T 312 253 0594) in Burnham & Root's (see p072) 1891 Monadnock Building (53 W Jackson Boulevard), cross the river into Greektown, and head up Halsted Street to the old meatpacking district (see p050). Turn onto Washington Boulevard for galleries Kavi Gupta (see p026) and Andrew Rafacz (see p066).

Do not miss the architectural treats away from the centre, either. There's a highly impressive ensemble on The University of Chicago campus (see p084). And you should catch the Green Line south to 35th-Bronzeville-IIT, for contemporary projects by Rem Koolhaas and Helmut Jahn (see p029), or west to Oak Park, for a three-hour tour (daily at noon; book in advance at www.flwright.org) of an incredible inventory of properties by Frank Lloyd Wright.
For full addresses, see Resources.

10.00 The Peninsula Spa

In such a competitive hotel scene, even the esteemed Peninsula (see p016) could not afford to rest on its laurels without risking a fall. Which explains why, within five years of the launch in the early noughties, the in-house spa underwent a rejig to turn it into one of the city's most attractive urban retreats. The serene space occupies the top two floors of the building. The reception and treatment areas are both wrapped in wood, a state-of-the-art gym surveys Lake Michigan from on high, and the 25m pool (above) has floor-to-ceiling windows and is the longest in any downtown hotel. There is a summer terrace, a yoga studio and a wide-ranging therapy list too. A visit here provides a relaxing start or end to the day; it stays open until 10pm (8pm on Sundays). *108 E Superior Street, T 312 573 6860, chicago.peninsula.com*

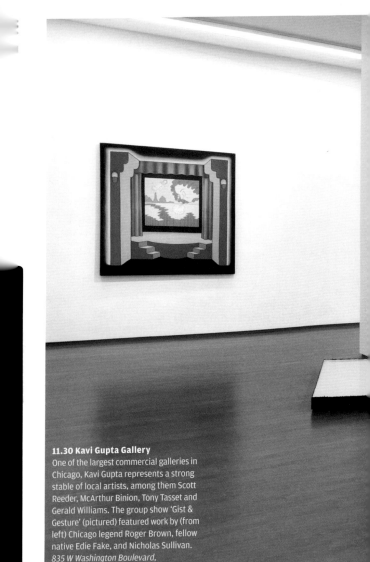

11.30 Kavi Gupta Gallery

One of the largest commercial galleries in Chicago, Kavi Gupta represents a strong stable of local artists, among them Scott Reeder, McArthur Binion, Tony Tasset and Gerald Williams. The group show 'Gist & Gesture' (pictured) featured work by (from left) Chicago legend Roger Brown, fellow native Edie Fake, and Nicholas Sullivan.
835 W Washington Boulevard,
T 312 432 0708, www.kavigupta.com

13.30 The Publican/Quality Meats

Now a cornerstone of the Fulton Market scene (see p034), The Publican is a meat and seafood lover's paradise (although don't come here expecting surf 'n' turf), specialising in oysters, pork and beer. If you haven't time for a proper exploration of the expansive menu and drinks lists, next-door sister venue Publican Quality Meats (above; T 312 445 8977) serves simplified versions of most dishes until 6pm (5pm on Sundays), to eat in or take away. But it would be a shame to miss out on the full monty. The communal walnut-wood seating and dozens of lights create an ambience that's part banquet hall, part gastropub. Order the charcuterie platter, sliced porchetta or bouchot mussels, and you will understand the glowing reviews.
837 W Fulton Market, T 312 733 9555, www.thepublicanrestaurant.com

16.00 Tribune Campus, IIT

Mies van der Rohe put his money where his mouth was during his 20-year tenure as director of architecture at the Illinois Institute of Technology, by designing its campus. However, by the mid-1990s, the IIT began to understand that man cannot live on (or in) Mies alone. Student numbers were down and the college was in need of a contemporary shot in the arm. Enter Rem Koolhaas, who won the contest to create the McCormick Tribune Campus Center. He devised a long, low building, seemingly squashed by the L train tracks overhead, which are wrapped in a 160m corrugated steel-and-concrete tube. IIT commissioned local firm Helmut Jahn for the State Street Village dorms. Strung along the side of the L, the raw concrete and glass blocks are punctuated by light-filled courtyards.
3300 S Federal Street, www.iit.edu

20.00 Elske

Husband-and-wife team David and Anna Posey — formerly of Blackbird (T 312 715 0708), known for its inventive Midwestern cuisine — opened Elske, which means 'love' in Danish, in 2016. The concept of *hygge* informs everything they do. Highly creative dishes like crispy veal sweetbreads with charred apricot, honey, mint and radish, and chilled zucchini and buttermilk cream with braised pistachio, blueberries and elderflower, have a Nordic soul, and are served on earthy, handmade ceramics by local Jessica Egan. The decor, by Boone Interiors, is similarly cosy: raw brickwork, darkwood tables, bronze fixtures, and art by David's brother Mark and others in the bar (right). Of the four signature cocktails, we like the Stirred, made with rye whisky, peach, Cynar and black-tea bitters; it's best enjoyed in front of the courtyard fireplace. *1350 W Randolph Street, T 312 733 1314, www.elskerestaurant.com*

URBAN LIFE

CAFÉS, RESTAURANTS, BARS AND NIGHTCLUBS

Foodies won't suffer in Chicago but dieters will struggle. The city is bristling with talented chefs. The most celebrated is molecular gastronomy master Grant Achatz, whose restaurant Alinea (see p044) garnered three Michelin stars in 2010; Achatz also heads up cocktail den Aviary (955 W Fulton Market, T 312 226 0868) and, on the same street, casual and fantastic Roister (No 951) and concept-shifting Next (No 953, T 312 226 0858). Other kitchen heroes are Stephanie Izard (see p034) and Rick Bayless (see p042). We're also fans of Donnie Madia and Paul Kahan, who are responsible for a slew of brilliant venues including Big Star (1531 N Damen Avenue, T 773 235 4039), a taco joint modelled on the South-west honky-tonks of the 1930s and 1940s, The Publican (see p028) and Avec (615 W Randolph Street, T 312 377 2002), a hit for the ambience, the design and the quality of the small plates. Giving them a run for their money in Fulton Market is Brendan Sodikoff (see p050).

Chicago has great neighbourhood spots too. In Pilsen, all-day Pleasant House Pub (2119 S Halsted Street, T 773 523 7437) does homemade pies and beer very well, Maria's Packaged Goods (960 W 31st Street, T 773 890 0588) in Bridgeport serves terrific cocktails, and Anteprima (5316 N Clark Street, T 773 506 9990) is a classic Italian in Andersonville. In Logan Square, check out Fat Rice (2957 W Diversey Avenue, T 773 661 9170), an upscale Macanese. *For full addresses, see Resources.*

Smyth and The Loyalist

Fine-diner Smyth (above) and The Loyalist, a casual lounge downstairs, are run by husband-and-wife team John and Karen Shields. The Michelin-starred restaurant offers either five-, eight- or 12-course menus inspired by the fresh produce and herbs mostly sourced from a farm near Bourbonnais. Imaginative dishes, such as brioche doughnut with aged beef au jus; grilled plants and squash with rice and pumpkin seeds; and roasted squab with sorrel, roses and *huitlacoche*, arrive on tableware from Portland-based Lilith Rockett. The Loyalist serves refined bar food with sparky flavours, and cocktails, like The Good Son Caliban (rye whisky, apple brandy, lemon, Fernet-Branca, egg white and soda), have a similar gearing.
177 N Ada Street, T 773 913 3773, www.smythandtheloyalist.com

Duck Duck Goat

Stephanie Izard has built a reputation as the mastermind behind some of Chicago's most inventive cuisine. In 2010, she opened Girl & The Goat (T 312 492 6262), serving up innovative small plates in the Fulton Market/meatpacking district. Little Goat (T 312 888 3455), Izard's diner over the road, is a light, bright antidote, which puts an imaginative spin on comfort food. Both are a culinary win-win. Her next spot, Duck

Duck Goat, offering Chinese fare, was no exception. Local produce is key, and the menu consists of elevated staples (egg rolls, wonton soup, fried rice) and more adventurous dishes (beef slap noodles with short-rib ragu and *luobo* radish). There is a cool Chinatown vibe infused with just the right level of kitsch.
857 W Fulton Market, T 312 902 3825, www.duckduckgoatchicago.com

Honey's

Housed in Fulton Market, inside a former machine shop, Honey's brings innovative, modern Mediterranean cooking – with a Midwest bent – to the West Loop. The kitchen sends out upscale, vibrant plates, such as Chefs Creek oysters with mango vinegar, shaved macadamia and mint, or a jerk-spiced pork chop served with cheddar grits, roasted kohlrabi and cherry relish. Start with something from the cocktail list, which uses funky ingredients, including tepache and sour cherry shrub, or a beer from local brewery Moody Tongue (T 312 600 5111). The breezy venue features a custom-designed quartzite bar, and an adjacent 60-seat dining room is flanked by creamy leather banquettes, with oak furniture and white linens. Evenings only. *1111 W Lake Street, T 312 877 5929, www.honeyschicago.com*

Estereo

Behind a roll-up garage door, Estereo's all about its convivial triangular bar and art deco-esque tiling, and exudes the aura of an old saloon. It's a hip, relaxed joint, and evenings are often set to a soundtrack of Latin American tunes. The drinks list, split into sections for pisco, cachaça, rum and mezcal, and the neat cocktails, follow suit. The Breezy mixes your choice of spirit with yerba mate, falernum, soda and lime, or try the wheat beer by Chicago brewer Off Color (T 773 687 8245) with jalapeno-infused tequila and blackberry; coffee, from local micro-roaster Four Letter Word, is decent too. It's open from 11am to 2am. The team also runs Pub Royale (T 773 661 6874) in Wicker Park, which purveys fine ales and Indian food (and somehow pulls this off). *2450 N Milwaukee Avenue, T 773 360 8363, www.estereochicago.com*

Proxi

Restaurateur Emmanuel Nony and chef Andrew Zimmerman first partnered up in 2007 when they established Michelin-starred Sepia (T 312 441 1920). Ten years later the duo opened Proxi, just a stone's throw from its sibling in a high-ceilinged former office building overhauled by New York practice Meyer Davis. It's a handsome space featuring geometric tile flooring, a white marble-top bar, artwork by painter Adrian Kay Wong and illustrator Félicie Haymoz, and custom dome pendants and sconces by Brooklyn-based firm Juniper. Zimmerman excels at refined, globally inspired street food: we had burrata with artichokes; corn on the cob tempura; raw tuna with coconut milk, lemongrass and ginger sorbet; and Wagyu short-rib curry. *565 W Randolph Street, T 312 466 1950, www.proxichicago.com*

Parson's Chicken & Fish

In a city where the weather can be harsh, comfort food goes down well. Parson's Chicken & Fish was launched by the folks behind happening Longman & Eagle (T 773 276 7110), and dishes up good old fried fare as per the name, accompanied by high-octane cocktails. Despite the hipsters who amass outside at the weekend, the venue is generally an oasis in Logan Square, with a back patio for summertime slumming (you can play tabletennis or bocce out there) and a punchy interior to help allay the winter blues. Order a basket of lightly battered familiarity and a cold beer, and settle in. There are lighter options on the menu too (small-plate greens, east and west coast oysters and a superb chickpea salad with feta cheese and pea shoots). *2952 W Armitage Avenue, T 773 384 3333, www.parsonschickenandfish.com*

Parachute

A hit for its sophisticated, Michelin-starred Korean-meets-the-US cuisine, Parachute puts an emphasis on conviviality: from the service to the home-style, produce-driven dishes, which are intended to be shared. The offering changes depending on what owners Beverly Kim and Johnny Clark can source, such as hearts of palm from Puna Gardens in Hawaii or dry-aged beef from Slagel Family Farm in Illinois. The menu might include raw yellowfin tuna with heirloom tomatoes and horseradish oil, or crispy squid and leek pancake with trout roe. The neat wine list is focused on natural, small-batch makers. Charlie Vinz jazzed up the low-key Avondale spot with multi-hued bar stools, and curtains crafted from parachutes, of course.
*3500 N Elston Avenue, T 773 654 1460,
www.parachuterestaurant.com*

Cruz Blanca

Rick Bayless' local Mexican institutions are legendary, and Cruz Blanca is enticing on two fronts, being both a *cervecería* and a taqueria: a gastropub with a Oaxacan twist. Jacob Sembrano is responsible for the beers, many of which riff on Mexico City's 19th-century brewing legacy – new-world interpretations of German, Austrian and French styles – and there are also funky US craft blends. Tacos come with a choice of *tasajo* (half-cured beef flank), chicken, chilli-marinated pork, chorizo or portobello mushroom, accompanied by wood-grilled onions, peppers and prickly pear cactus, smoky *pasilla* sauce and avocado salsa. Next-door sister spot Leña Brava is more formal and majors on Bajan dishes, notably fire-cooked seafood, and fine mezcals.
904 W Randolph Street, T 312 733 1975, www.rickbayless.com

Alinea
Since Grant Achatz and Nick Kokonas launched Alinea in 2005, it has received so many plaudits that it's hard to believe this establishment lives up to the hype, but it does. In 2016 the elaborate multi-course menus and interiors underwent a stylish revamp. This is modern haute cuisine at its finest, and there is still no restaurant in the country quite like it.
1723 N Halsted Street, T 312 867 0110

Terzo Piano

On the third floor of the Art Institute of Chicago (see p074), hence the name, this Italian/Mediterranean restaurant was given a glossy update in 2017 by original architects Dirk Denison. The firm added a reception anchored by a white marble bar and lit by Eileen Gray's 'Tube Light', and chairs by Patricia Urquiola, Arne Jacobsen and David Adjaye for Knoll. The sculptures in glass vitrines are by Nairy Baghramian.

The kitchen is overseen by Tony Mantuano, partner at Spiaggia (T 312 280 2750), and chef Carolina Diaz, who sources produce from the Midwest in dishes such as grilled swordfish with fregula sarda, prosciutto and sorrel, and spaghetti with tuna crudo, bottarga, green onions and pepper cream. In summer, ask to be seated on the terrace. *159 E Monroe Street, T 312 443 8650, www.terzopianochicago.com*

Bavette's Bar & Boeuf

It may be a modern take on the classic Chicago steakhouse, but Bavette's interior is more reminiscent of Musso & Frank, the legendary Hollywood restaurant. No wonder, as the retro decor is rooted in the Roaring Twenties. It's another triumph for Brendan Sodikoff (see p050), alongside Gilt Bar (T 312 464 9544), Maude's Liquor Bar (T 312 243 9712) and Au Cheval (T 312 929 4580). The hors d'oeuvres menu is packed with seafood and salads, but the main event is the meat, naturally. You can't go wrong with the classic bone-in ribeye or filet mignon (petite duchess cut) with roasted tomato, herb butter and cracked pepper. To wash it down, there's an ample selection of bourbon, whisky, scotch and beer, as well as bubbly cocktails.

218 W Kinzie Street, T 312 624 8154, www.bavetteschicago.com

Income Tax
High-spirited, casual yet stylish Income Tax is a little off piste but well worth the trip. The kitchen delivers European-led small plates, and the wine list focuses on old-world labels and small producers. The cocktails are superb too – the house option, which inspired the name of the bar, blends gin, Cocchi Americano, red vermouth, orange juice and bitters.
5959 N Broadway, T 773 897 9165

Green Street Smoked Meats

While most of the longtime meatpackers that populated the Fulton Market/West Loop area have vacated to make room for development (while lining their pockets), one place you can still experience the city's butchering history is at this Texas-style BBQ joint, one of a number of restaurants run by Brendan Sodikoff, well-known for his line-creating burger at Au Cheval (see p047) up the street. The meat here has a healthy amount of rub, and portions, from the pulled-pork sandwich to sliced brisket, ribs and pastrami, are generous. The vibe is deliberately casual; it is set in a former warehouse with corrugated iron walls and bar, scratched paint and long picnic tables, part-illuminated by fairy lights. Sodikoff's High Five Ramen is down in the basement. *112 N Green Street, T 312 754 0431, www.greenstreetmeats.com*

Billy Sunday

Before his name was commandeered by one of the city's best craft cocktail bars, Billy Sunday was a baseball player in the late 19th century, who found God at the Pacific Garden Mission and became an advocate of prohibition. The venue was set up by Matthias Merges, who owns French/Italian restaurant A10 (T 773 288 1010) and worked with chef Charlie Trotter. Together with his wife, Rachel Crowl, who conceived the 1940s-inspired interior, Merges has created a laidback locale in Logan Square. The cocktails are the headline event, and they tend to lean towards the sweet, Southern side of the spectrum. This place comes into its own in winter: cosied up here with a nightcap is an ideal way to see out a bitterly cold day. *3143 W Logan Boulevard, T 773 661 2485, www.billy-sunday.com*

Boeufhaus

A vivacious alternative to the traditional starched linen and mahogany steakhouses that are dotted all over town, this French/German-inspired brasserie is distinct for its smallish size and simple decor of white subway tiles, high butcher-block tables and a copper and red oak bar. The steaks and chops are prime – beef from Creekstone, and pork and lamb from Catalpa Farms in Dwight – which you should pair with a crisp house martini. The accompaniments are understated yet also of a high quality: salmon crudo is plated with radish, grape, fennel and sea bean, and there's a delicate cauliflower gratin. Boeufhaus is committed to sustainability, responsible rearing and artisanal ingredients, and service is equally fresh and genuine. The small counter at the front operates as a speciality butcher.
1012 N Western Avenue, T 773 661 2116, www.boeufhaus.com

INSIDER'S GUIDE

STEVEN HAULENBEEK, DESIGNER

Designer Steven Haulenbeek (see p068) moved here from Michigan in 2004 to study at the Art Institute (see p074). 'Chicago is a huge but liveable city,' he says. 'It has the hustle of bigger metropolises, but retains a laidback Midwest attitude.' It suits his practice, which spans sculpture, lighting and furniture: 'As someone who makes things, this is a great place to live. It's a major manufacturing hub.'

His 'go-to spot', near his Logan Square studio, is all-day Lula Cafe (2537 N Kedzie Boulevard, T 773 489 9554), run by chef Jason Hammel, which serves farm-to-table US fare: 'The atmosphere is slightly cool, but it's casual.' In the evenings, he might visit Duck Duck Goat (see p034) for a 'unique take on Chinese cuisine' or Parson's Chicken & Fish (see p040): 'Its patio is rivalled only by Big Star (see p032).' He enjoys Avec (see p032) for the service and 'delicious food', and the tempting dishes at next-door Blackbird (see p030). He also recommends the three-Michelin-starred Grace (652 W Randolph Street, T 312 234 9494), for its handsome interior and exquisite tasting menus (the 'Flora' caters for vegetarians).

On nights out, Haulenbeek usually frequents low-key bars, like Danny's Tavern (1951 W Dickens Avenue, T 773 489 6457), where 'you can dance your ass off', or he'll settle in at cool neighbourhood spot The Charleston (2076 N Hoyne Avenue, T 773 489 4757): 'I've spent the majority of my birthdays there for the last decade.'
For full addresses, see Resources.

ART AND DESIGN
GALLERIES, STUDIOS AND PUBLIC SPACES

The heavyweight Art Institute of Chicago (see p074) dates back to 1893, but it wasn't until the 1960s that attention was really paid to the contemporary scene, when Richard Gray (opposite) and the MCA (see p060) opened. In the 1980s, the creative set moved in to River North, and it remains vibrant: visit Zolla Lieberman (325 W Huron Street, T 312 944 1990) to discover the latest names. Next came West Loop, where Kavi Gupta (see p026) and Andrew Rafacz (see p066) led the charge. Wicker Park has been a hotbed since the early noughties, due to the arrival of Monique Meloche (see p063) and Corbett vs Dempsey (see p070). Today, art is a significant part of the urban fabric, through public sculpture (see p067), graffiti, wheatpaste signs and projects like Matthew Hoffman's 'You Are Beautiful' messages, while local hero Theaster Gates has launched a community initiative, Stony Island Arts Bank (6760 S Stony Island Avenue, T 312 857 5561), in the disadvantaged South Side.

There is an insatiable appetite for midcentury design here (see p064), but a flock of new-wave talent is forging a fresh agenda still imbued with a heritage feel – the work of Casey Lurie (see p059) is one example, as is the practice of Norman Kelley, whose Aesop store (1653 N Damen Avenue, T 872 802 4626) interior, done out in gridded brick, is worth the trip alone. Volume (see p062) shows the young guns, like Sung Jang (see p092) and Thomas Leinberger. *For full addresses, see Resources.*

Richard Gray Gallery

Founded in 1963, Richard Gray has long been a major force in the contemporary art scene, and the roster packs quite a punch: David Hockney, Bethany Collins, Alex Katz and Rashid Johnson. And then there's Chicago's favourite son Theaster Gates, whose 2016 'Heavy Sketches' show featured sculptures in bronze and mixed materials based on West African masks. In addition to its regular home within the Hancock Building (T 312 642 8877), the gallery opened this expansive site in 2017, set in a former machine shop overhauled by local firm Wheeler Kearns, who restored the wood-truss ceiling and added concrete floors. It is handy for hosting large-scale works, for example neo-Dadaist Jim Dine's paintings ('Looking at the Present', above). *2004 W Carroll Avenue, T 312 883 8277, www.richardgraygallery.com*

Document

This small and edgy gallery – a simple, lo-fi venue with white walls, lightwood floors and industrial elements – specialises in photography, film and media-based art. Founded in 2011 by Aron Gent, it focuses on bringing new and emerging names to wider attention. A 2017 joint exhibition by local talents John Paul Morabito and Laura Letinsky saw them combine photography and weaving in painterly cotton and wool works, while John Opera showed a range of compelling geometric cyanotypes in 'Technical Images' (above). There is a coterie of fresh enterprises in the building, which is the hub of the Ukrainian Village scene – Volume Gallery (see p062), Paris London Hong Kong (see p069) and Western Exhibitions (T 312 480 8390) are all here. *1709 W Chicago Avenue, T 262 719 3500, www.documentspace.com*

Casey Lurie

Southern California-born Casey Lurie launched his studio in 2012, following a stint at Idée, a Tokyo-based furniture manufacturer, and graduate study at Northwestern University in Chicago. A Japanese influence is manifest in his exquisitely put-together, robust-looking furniture, such as the 'Primo' shelving system, in which ash, walnut or white oak boards interlock without screws, assembled instead with brass brackets that add a midcentury accent. The 'Taut' chair (above) draws from the curved seat usually seen in a traditional Windsor chair; this lithe, handsome piece is constructed by heat-stretching leather, sourced from local tannery Horween, over stainless-steel rods. It is then hand-stitched into place. Visit the studio by appointment. *T 312 804 2964, www.caseylurie.com*

Museum of Contemporary Art

Established in 1967, the MCA continues to put on a dynamic, provocative programme. The headline shows by Takashi Murakami, Thomas Ruff et al draw the crowds, but an ongoing project, Chicago Works, focuses on native talent, including painter Paul Heyer and sculptor Diane Simpson, and there are more than 2,500 pieces dating back to the 1920s in the permanent collection. The museum moved to this rather imposing, classically proportioned, aluminium-clad new-build, by German architect Josef Paul Kleihues, in 1996. A 2017 interior overhaul by LA-based Johnston Marklee includes a hanging garden installation by Mexicans Pedro&Juana and a vibrant mural by Brit Chris Ofili inside restaurant Marisol (T 312 799 3599), helmed by Sarah Rinkavage. *220 E Chicago Avenue, T 312 280 2660, www.mcachicago.org*

Volume Gallery

Sam Vinz and Claire Warner met working at Richard Wright (see p064), and launched Volume in order to promote contemporary US designers in 2010. Initially an itinerant project, it settled first in West Loop, then West Town amid a clutch of other galleries (see p058) in 2017. The duo seek out fresh creatives who, in their view, are helping to shape a new language by escaping the 'long shadow cast by the 20th-century

greats'. Pieces on display are frequently limited edition and produced locally. Past exhibitors have included Felicia Ferrone, Norman Kelley, Matthias Merkel Hess and Michael C Andrews ('Tuft', above), who presented a variety of large, tapestry-like works crafted from wool. These squiggly forms straddle textile art and sculpture.
1709 W Chicago Avenue,
T 312 666 7954, www.wvolumes.com

Monique Meloche Gallery

Influential gallerist Monique Meloche has long been a Chicago figurehead. She was formerly a curator at the MCA (see p060), and also worked for Kavi Gupta (see p026) and the highly respected Rhona Hoffman (T 312 455 1990). She established this sleek space, with glossed concrete flooring and a clutch of different rooms, in 2001. It is one of the largest, smartest commercial offerings in the city, supporting a dynamic roster of close to 20 artists, many local, including Cheryl Pope, Nate Young, Dan Gunn and Karen Reimer. Group show 'A New Look' (above) featured work by Sadie Barnette (left), Jillian Mayer (on plinth) and Zoë Charlton (right). In 2011, Meloche also organised the inaugural Gallery Weekend, which now takes place every November.
2154 W Division Street, T 773 252 0299, www.moniquemeloche.com

Wright Gallery

Some of the rarest pieces of modernist design find their way to this West Loop warehouse, before being redistributed under the hammer to a widely flung community of collectors. Here you can bid for a Robert Mallet-Stevens chair, a Poul Kjærholm coffee table, or even a Pierre Koenig Case Study House – items that fetch huge sums and are right at the heart of the 'Is it art/Is it design?' debate. Created by Richard Wright in a one-time printers, the venue has been adapted to the business. Lots arrive through a roll-up garage door, are transferred to a photo studio to be documented, then moved to the display area (right). On auction days, a café is set up in the mezzanine viewing gallery – peer over the side and you will spy spectacular midcentury furnishings stacked in the storage room.
1440 W Hubbard Street, T 312 563 0020, www.wright20.com

Andrew Rafacz

This eponymous, spirited venue promotes emerging and mid-career artists, many of them Chicago-based, such as Samantha Bittman, whose pieces combine textiles with painting, and multimedia talent Cody Hudson (aka Struggle Inc). Robert Burnier's 'So That Justice Should Be Tyrant' show (above) consisted of a series of dynamic, intimate sculptures crafted from sheet metal. High-quality group presentations are also a regular fixture; 'Figured Out!' displayed vibrant, figurative ceramics by the likes of David Leggett and William J O'Brien, both locals. While rising rents have seen a number of other mid-level enterprises fly the West Loop coop, this low-key space has been a staple here since 2004. Closed Sunday and Monday. *835 W Washington Boulevard, T 312 404 9188, www.andrewrafacz.com*

Millennium Park

The most controversial of former mayor Richard M Daley's civic improvements, the 2004 Millennium Park was priced up at $150m. However, six years of construction ran the bill closer to an unearthly $500m, and resulted in several prison sentences for dodgy dealing. Yet few have criticised the end result. It is dominated by massive sculptural statements, the most famous of which is Anish Kapoor's seamless stainless-steel, bean-like *Cloud Gate* (above), which distorts the city around it. Elsewhere, the Catalan artist Jaume Plensa's wondrous *Crown Fountain* comprises a pair of glass towers, joined by a shallow pool, playing video portraits that intermittently spout water. Frank Gehry's Jay Pritzker Pavilion, an open-air auditorium, is also a favourite. The canopy of pipes and giant steel ribbons play perfectly to the architect's strengths.

Steven Haulenbeek

The tactile, industrial-inflected output of Steven Haulenbeek (see p054) melds sculpture and design. Much of his work is process-driven, such as the 'Ice-Cast' series, a collection of fantastical mirrors, tables and vases formed by pouring hot wax into a frozen mould, before casting the result in bronze. The 'Bully' table, which has a deceptively simple, origami-like form, is assembled from 17 laser-cut aluminium parts that are welded together and given a verdigris patina. The result of yet another experiment with materials, his coral- and cactus-esque 'RBS Vessels' ('#54', above) are made from textured, resin-bonded sand, and come in a rainbow of soft hues. Find pieces at Haute Living (T 312 329 9000) and Holly Hunt (T 312 661 1900) or visit the studio by appointment. *www.stevenhaulenbeek.com*

Devening Projects

Helmed by local artist Dan Devening, who is also co-director of Paris London Hong Kong (see p058), this low-key enterprise hosts a variety of edgy shows with a focus on site-specific works. The wide-ranging programme has included New Yorker Jason Karolak's wobbly, geometric canvases and Angharad Davies' video piece of re-filmed photographs taken while travelling, which explored the subject of memory. In 2017, Illinoisian Melissa Pokorny presented 'Call If You Need Me' (above), a collection of crafty, unwieldly installations and wall works. Chicago-based talent is celebrated too, such as painter Steven Husby, sculptor Allison Wade and multimedia exponent Mark Booth. It is open on Saturdays from 12pm to 5pm and by appointment.
3039 W Carroll Avenue, T 312 420 4720, www.deveningprojects.com

Corbett vs Dempsey

Established by John Corbett and Jim
Dempsey in 2004, CvsD specialises in
painting, sculpture and works on paper
from 1940 to the present. For example,
it has hosted a major retrospective on
the counterculture printmaker William
Weege, who was most active in the late
1960s and early 1970s, as well as Arlene
Shechet's colourful abstracts that often
reference body parts (*In the Meantime*,
pictured). The gallery also shows young
artists from the region, such as Magalie
Guérin's paintings and drawings, and
Molly Zuckerman-Hartung, who dyes
and bleaches canvas, nylon, cotton and
other materials. While you're here, drop
into Dusty Groove (T 773 342 5800), a
great record store on the ground floor.
*1120 N Ashland Avenue, T 773 278 1664,
www.corbettvsdempsey.com*

ARCHITOUR

A GUIDE TO CHICAGO'S ICONIC BUILDINGS

In 1871, much of the urban landscape was destroyed by fire. For a city already committed to challenging New York as the commercial (if not the cultural) epicentre of the nation, this at least provided Chicago with the chance to recreate itself with a new dynamism, and architects poured in from all over the country to be part of the project. Among them were Louis Henry Sullivan – who devised the maxim 'form follows function' – William Le Baron Jenney, Daniel Burnham and his partner John Root. They developed what became known as the Chicago School and designed the first skyscrapers here. Although these barely made it into double digits in terms of storeys, they were, in their steel-frame construction and stripping back of ornamentation, the technical parents of the giants to come.

The city seems to provide textbook illustrations of successive styles. It gave the world the vertical thrust of the high-rise and the horizontal planes of the Prairie School; it was the mother lode of modernism and then a PoMo playground. And these shifts from one movement to another now appear quite seamless. Of course, the development of the metropolis has always been the result of a fierce and chaotic conflict of approaches and interests, sometimes within the same building. Yet it was the quality of the competition that turned this place into the ideas factory in which 20th-century architecture was defined, and where it found its most perfect form. *For full addresses, see Resources.*

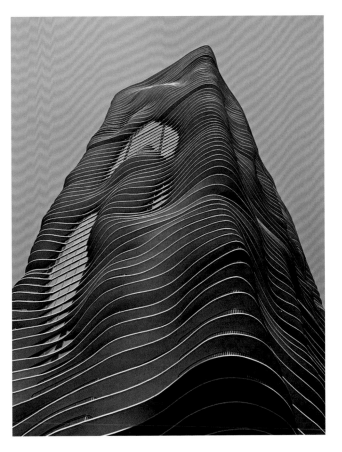

Aqua Tower

Since 2010 when this sculptural tower was unveiled, another 100 high-rises have shot up in Chicago, yet Aqua remains one of the city's most accomplished. Local architects Studio Gang were inspired by the layered Miners Castle karst rock formation on Lake Superior in creating its rippled, wave-like exterior. But it is not just a pretty facade. The sinuous balconies that wrap around its 82 storeys cantilever out to 4m, providing shading from the sun to improve energy efficiency, and negating the need for a weighted core due to the manner in which they are able to disperse the wind. The Radisson Blu (T 312 565 5258) occupies the lower 18 floors, the first three of which form a wide podium. On the top of this is a 7,400 sq m landscaped garden, replete with running track and swimming pool.
225 N Columbus Drive

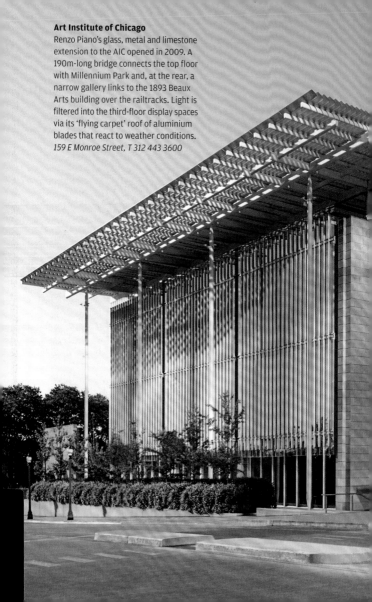

Art Institute of Chicago
Renzo Piano's glass, metal and limestone
extension to the AIC opened in 2009. A
190m-long bridge connects the top floor
with Millennium Park and, at the rear, a
narrow gallery links to the 1893 Beaux
Arts building over the railtracks. Light is
filtered into the third-floor display spaces
via its 'flying carpet' roof of aluminium
blades that react to weather conditions.
159 E Monroe Street, T 312 443 3600

Fisher Studio Houses

Still an incredibly successful splice of art deco flair and modernist mechanics, the 1936 Fisher Studio Houses were conceived by Andrew Rebori, a noted bon vivant who had useful relations with Chicago's social elite. The project was commissioned by Frank Fisher Jr, an executive at Marshall Field & Co. Fisher showed Rebori a very narrow plot and told him to get the most (upscale) apartments he could out of it.

Rebori devised a plan for 12 four-storey duplexes built around a courtyard, behind an elegant, rounded facade of whitewashed brick and glass blocks that's typical of the Depression Modern style, with sculptural flourishes by artist Edgar Miller. Indeed, there's a suspicion that Miller actually had a larger hand in the overall design, and it remains a thrilling composition face on.
1209 N State Parkway

Chase Tower

As many splendid buildings as there are in Chicago, there are also a fair few clunkers. Fortunately the symbolic central block of The Loop is occupied by one of the city's most idiosyncratic constructions. It was designed by CF Murphy Associates and Perkins + Will and completed in 1969, and christened Chase in 2005. A 265m-tall slab faced in granite, its intense visual drama is the result of a graceful sweep from the base, which starts at 61m wide, to the top, where it finishes up only half that. It is best viewed from the Skydeck in the Willis Tower (see p012). A two-storey sunken plaza to its south is adorned with Marc Chagall's *Four Seasons*, a mosaic rendered in 370 sq m of ceramic tiles. Its other claim to fame is that Barack and Michelle Obama met here while working at law firm Sidley Austin.
10 S Dearborn Street

Gary Comer Youth Center

In 1999, clothing mogul Gary Comer visited his old school in rundown Grand Crossing in the South Side, prompting him to fund maintenance work. Since then, Comer and his estate have poured a whopping $86m into the area, providing vaccinations for pupils and buying uniforms to eradicate gang colours, and constructing affordable housing, a school and, on the same street, this 2006 youth centre. Designed by local architect John Ronan, its whimsical, lego-like, cement-tile facade references the colours of the drill team. A performance space/gym caters for a diverse range of activities, and there are recording studios and a media lab. On the roof, a 2,500 sq m educational garden grows vegetables for the kitchen, which can feed 800 kids a day. *7200 S Ingleside Avenue, www.garycomeryouthcenter.org*

John Hancock Center

One practice, Skidmore, Owings & Merrill, has dominated corporate architecture in postwar America. Nowhere is that more evident than in this city. And no structure better typifies SOM's power slabs than the John Hancock Center, completed in 1970. Largely the work of Bruce Graham, along with engineers Fazlur Khan and Myron Goldsmith, the uncompromising zigzag trusses and black aluminium skin of the tapered, 344m-high, 100-storey colossus lend it a brooding, iconic force, and make it the definitive Chicago skyscraper. Its location marks one end of the Magnificent Mile and the open-air viewing deck on the 94th floor is arguably the finest place to drink in vistas of the urban milieu as well as an impressive portion of the Midwest. *875 N Michigan Avenue, T 312 751 3681, www.johnhancockcenterchicago.com*

Lake Point Tower

George Schipporeit and John Heinrich's 1968 high-rise is still one of the chicest addresses in town, and its presence is as compelling now as then. Essentially, the 70-storey tower has a triangular plan with bowed sides. All the supports and services are at the core, meaning that none of the promontories requires any interior load-bearing walls, which allows for complete freedom of design. Each apartment has a view of Lake Michigan but, thanks to the curvature of the windows, not of other residents' homes. The building also has a 10,000 sq m private park on the third floor, devised by the landscape architect Alfred Caldwell. It encompasses an outdoor swimming pool, a waterfall and a lagoon, manicured gardens and some 80 trees.
505 N Lake Shore Drive,
www.lakepointtower.org

Mansueto Library

Comprising almost 700 glass panels, the elliptical dome of local architect Helmut Jahn's 2011 library extension bulges out of the ground to flood its reading room with light. Storage is subterranean, and there is a capacity for three and a half million volumes, which are retrieved by robots. A glazed corridor links to the 1970 brutalist original (above, right), which could not be more different, by the legendary Chicago architect Walter Netsch of SOM. His five Neolithic-looking buildings are a mass of variously sized, loosely packed blocks, clad in ridged limestone that resembles pages. Next door, Ricardo Legorreta's 2001 red-brick student accommodation (above, left) incorporates his signature bright pastels on the window cladding, and is another hit on this strikingly eclectic campus (overleaf). *1100 E 57th Street*

Logan Center for the Arts

Bordering Midway Plaisance park, this 2012 new-build by Tod Williams and Billie Tsien houses The University of Chicago faculties of visual and performing arts, music and film all in one venue. Constructed in multi-hued Missouri limestone, it comprises two elements. A low-slung, understated volume references the Midwest prairies, and hosts artists' studios beneath a sawtooth roof of north-facing skylights, as well as theatres and practice rooms below. The 10-storey tower is a nod to the city's skyscrapers and the neo-Gothic spires nearby. A variety of recital and exhibition spaces include the top floor, which has views to The Loop and the lake. Robie House (opposite) and Mansueto Library (see p082) are also on campus, which is a 15-minute train ride from Millennium Station to 59th Street. *915 E 60th Street, T 773 702 2787*

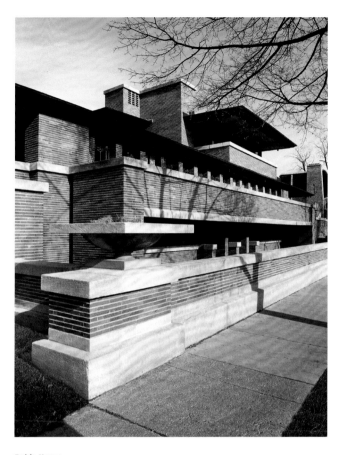

Robie House

Frank Lloyd Wright's most fully realised Prairie Style house was completed in 1910. Entrepreneur Frederick Robie had requested as modern a home as possible. But Wright's holistic design – the interior and exterior were conceived to be totally integrated – was simply revolutionary, not least in having burglar alarms, a central vacuum system and a connected garage. Everything reinforces the horizontal plane, from the bands of limestone and brick to the balconies and cantilevered roofs. The serene open-plan living room, dapled with light through stained-glass windows, is furnished with bespoke pieces by Wright, including high-backed chairs and a dining table with inbuilt lights. The weekend tours last longer. Closed Tuesday and Wednesday. *5757 S Woodlawn Avenue, T 312 994 4000, www.flwright.org*

Eleanor Boathouse at Park 571
Studio Gang's second boathouse (the first
is in Clark Park) opened in 2016 as part of
an ongoing regeneration project dubbed
'Building on Burnham' (Daniel Burnham
drafted Chicago's masterplan in 1909).
One aim is to beautify every stretch of
river, and add pedestrian crossings and
cycle paths. This is exemplified by 2016's
Riverwalk, a 2.4km promenade along East
Lower Wacker Drive, led by local firm Ross
Barney with landscape architects Sasaki
Associates. The hope is that such stylish
boathouses will encourage the city's youth,
traditionally obsessed with basketball and
baseball, to take up rowing. The sculptural
roof here – a series of structural trusses
fitted with skylights – mimics the motion
and rhythm of the sport. The facility is clad
in zinc, with a ripple-effect gradated wall.
2828 S Eleanor Street, T 773 823 9135

SHOPS

THE BEST RETAIL THERAPY AND WHAT TO BUY

While there might be a paucity of sophisticated local retail concepts here, Chicago still provides interesting shopping opportunities. The city has become a mecca for enthusiasts of midcentury design (see p064 and p094), and a competitive restaurant culture has put a slew of upscale delicatessens on the agenda; we'd suggest Olivia's Market (2014 W Wabansia Avenue, T 773 227 4220). Then there's a healthy coffee scene in which Intelligentsia (see p024) rules the roast, but we also like to take home the nicely packaged beans by Metropolis (1039 W Granville Avenue, T 773 764 0400).

There are handy clusters dotted around the city. On the north side of W Fulton Street is a strip of design emporiums, including Morlen Sinoway Atelier (1052 W Fulton Market, T 312 432 0100), with more along W Grand Avenue (see p094). In the Ukrainian Village, Circa Modern (1114 N Ashland Avenue, T 773 697 9239) is a vintage treasure trove. International brands can be found in the wallet-weakening Oak Street corridor. For something a little more homespun, browse Wicker Park's independent fashion stores, like Moon Voyage (2010 W Pierce Avenue, T 773 423 8853), and Logan Square, where you will find Tusk (3205 W Armitage Avenue, T 423 903 7093) – both offer a well-edited range of womenswear. And head to the south end of The Loop for one-off bookstores, such as the hip Curbside (125 S Clark Street), which sells records too.
For full addresses, see Resources.

Martha Mae

Named after owner Jean Cate's Cavalier King Charles spaniel, who is frequently in residence, Martha Mae purveys design objects, art supplies and good-looking things for the home, from sterling silver bookmarks by Wms & Co to sculptural vases by Andrew Jessup, porcelain vessels from Christie Chapin and a selection of coffee-table books. Cate's watercolours, etchings and drawings are also for sale.

Behind a bright-pink facade, the breezy store is fitted out with maplewood tables and shelves with brass fixtures. The items on display make lovely souvenirs or gifts, which staff will wrap in Japanese paper on request. While you are in the area, stop by Norcross and Scott (T 773 564 9533) around the corner for more stylish housewares.
5407 N Clark Street, T 872 806 0988, www.marthamae.info

Gallery Aesthete
Opened in 2012 by Stephen Naparstek, this sleek showroom designed by Lukas Machnik displays a well-curated edit of avant-garde menswear from cult labels such as Boris Bidjan Saberi, Damir Doma and Julius. Then there are accessories like Lee Brennan jewellery, plus Mad et Len fragrances, and rotating artworks by Lonney White III, Fraser Taylor et al. *1751 W Division Street, T 312 265 1883*

Sung Jang

A graduate of Milan's Domus Academy and the School of the Art Institute of Chicago, designer Sung Jang's studies in fine arts and sculpture inform his practice. The '03 Stool' (above), from $800, is part of his 'Comb Pattern' collection. A supporter of the city's manufacturing heritage, he used a milling technique that creates unique patterns on the seat; available in a variety of hardwoods. We also like the 'Plyform Lamp', which has a red cord that provides a punchy contrast to its slender silhouette. Socially aware, Jang devised a cheap solar-powered LED lamp that can be installed in a piece of scrap wood with a plastic bottle-top diffuser, to help eliminate the need for kerosene lanterns in the developing world. Volume Gallery (see p062) carries select pieces, or visit his studio by appointment. *www.sungjanglaboratory.com*

Mint Home

After starting out as an online business, Mint Home opened this bricks-and-mortar venture in 2012. It's a bijou store with an authentic pressed-tin ceiling and retro light fixtures. Owners Jessie Kuhny and Keisha Bandealy scour the Midwest for largely midcentury pieces (Danish sofas, vintage dressers, teak credenzas and oversized brass planters) to fill their boutique. Living up to the name, each item is thoughtfully refurbished back to its original condition at a workshop in Ravenswood. There's a mix of contemporary objects too, from natural bath products by Ænon to Hook and Stem serving boards and an array of products made by local artisans. A couple of blocks away, Mint Mini (T 312 504 6111) caters for kids' spaces. Closed Monday and Tuesday. *2117 W Irving Park Road, T 773 292 6369, www.minthomechicago.com*

Modern Times

Occupying a vast brick-walled warehouse,
Modern Times is at the western edge of the
burgeoning Grand Avenue Design District.
Martha Torno and Tom Clark established
their gallery of 20th-century pieces back
in 1991, and the hoard remains as strong
as ever. Rich in US midcentury modern
lighting, ceramics and furnishings, this
impressive collection is low on clichés
and high on more unusual or surprising
finds, including items by under-the-radar
creatives and artisanal work that has been
produced in the Chicago area. Everything
offered for sale is in tip-top condition, so
it is well worth heading out here. A passion
for vintage accessories is reflected in the
couple's sideline in handbags sourced on
their travels (www.modbag.com).
2100 W Grand Avenue, T 312 243 5706,
www.moderntimeschicago.com

ESCAPES

WHERE TO GO IF YOU WANT TO LEAVE TOWN

Despite Chicago's status as one of the world's busiest aviation hubs, few think of it as a base for shorter jaunts. This is despite the fact that much of the surrounding country is not the flat, grassy prairie of legend, but rather hills and beaches, sand dunes and great pine forests. It is no accident that immigrant Scandinavians have found such comfort in the local landscape. Visitors have four states to explore: Illinois, Michigan, Wisconsin and Indiana, each with its own particular and peculiar history. Berrien County, 150km to the north-east, has become a focal point for Michigan's surprisingly rich viticulture. Nearby Harbor Country boasts the upmarket New Buffalo lakeside resort. Madison, Wisconsin's capital, is known for its 260 parks, five lakes, 10 beaches, fine food, vigorous cultural life and all-round liveability. And it's just 240km away.

The Midwest also does a lovely line in manmade attractions, as the architectural energy that was expended on Chicago spread out into the hinterland. Seek out Mies' impeccable Farnsworth House (see p102) in Plano, Frank Lloyd Wright's monumental efforts in Racine (see p098), and the unique result of corporate benevolence in Columbus (see p100). If those were not enough, Milwaukee Art Museum (opposite) is a contemporary gem. Apart from Columbus, all can be reached in not more than 90 minutes. And you thought this place had little to offer apart from beer and *Laverne & Shirley*. *For full addresses, see Resources.*

Milwaukee Art Museum

Partly housed in a Eero Saarinen building, and an adjoining structure by David Kahler, MAM received this eye-catching addition in 2001. Its shiny white steel form resembles a ship at full mast, and makes for a striking contrast to the existing ensemble. Architect Santiago Calatrava incorporated a pair of signature wings that span 65m, comprising expansive louvres that form a moveable brise-soleil – catch it in action at the 10am opening, noon, and 5pm closing (8pm on Thursday); note that it shuts automatically in strong winds. Inside, Windhover Hall (above) mimics a Gothic cathedral (flying buttresses, pointed arches, ribbed vaults and a central nave). The collection of more than 30,000 works includes a large haul of paintings by Wisconsinite Georgia O'Keeffe.
700 N Art Museum Drive, Milwaukee,
T 414 224 3200, www.mam.org

Johnson Wax Building, Racine

Despite a reputation as a huge, if irascible, talent, Frank Lloyd Wright was struggling for work in the mid-1930s. He was rescued by HF Johnson Jr of SC Johnson, the wax people, who commissioned him to devise new offices, and a mansion, in the lakeside town of Racine, Wisconsin. Completed in 1939, the commercial premises is a squat, corporate-sized take on the Prairie Style, and it became known for its mushroom-like 9.5m-tall internal columns (opposite). Impressed, Johnson approached Wright again to design a research facility. He came up with a striped vertical counterpart in the shape of a 15-storey tower (above), opened in 1950, which remains a wonder to behold. There are 90-minute tours on Thursdays to Sundays, March to December. *1525 Howe Street, T 262 260 2154, www.scjohnson.com/company/visiting.aspx*

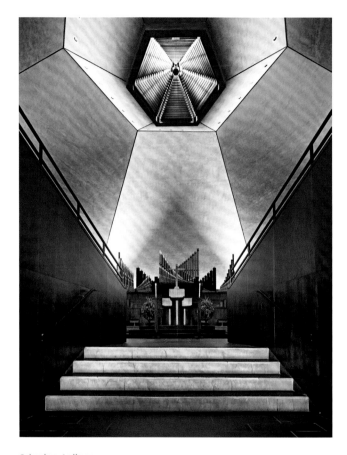

Columbus, Indiana

Despite having a population of just 46,000, Columbus has been anointed as the sixth-most architecturally significant city in the US. In 1957, the town's major employer, the Cummins Engine Company (helmed by J Irwin Miller, aka the 'Medici of the West'), decided it would cover the design fees for a whole host of public structures, as long as the protagonists were of international standing and modernist intent. There had been a precursor: Eero Saarinen's 1954 Irwin Union Bank, which broke the mould for finance buildings in America. To date, Columbus has more than 60 edifices of interest, including Saarinen's 1957 Miller House (opposite) and 1964 North Christian Church (above), as well as works by IM Pei, Robert Venturi and Deborah Berke. The Columbus Area Visitors Center (T 812 378 2622) has maps and runs various tours.

Miller House, Columbus

This family home, commissioned in 1953 by industrialist J Irwin and wife Xenia Simons Miller, is one of America's finest modernist residences – a collaboration by a trio of creative talents at the top of their game. Eero Saarinen's flowing grid-plan design, under a series of skylights, was enhanced by Alexander Girard's rich furnishings and layout, including the world's first lounge pit, an innovative 15m rosewood 'storage wall' (above), folk art pieces and bright customised textiles, from curtains to rugs and cushion covers. Landscape architect Dan Kiley created the exquisitely formed gardens, which feature an allée of delicate honey locust trees flanking the west of the house. The Columbus Area Visitors Center (opposite) offers 90-minute tours – you should book at least a month in advance. *www.columbus.in.us*

Farnsworth House, Plano

Mies van der Rohe never got more Miesian (or more grief) than he did for Farnsworth House, completed in 1951. The client was kidney specialist Dr Edith Farnsworth, who asked the architect to design her a house on a 25-hectare plot on the Fox River in Plano, Illinois. He came up with a sublime floating glazed box, measuring just 23.5m by 8.8m, held aloft by white steel I-beams. Not that Dr Farnsworth was content. She kicked Mies off the job with the interiors still unfinished, he filed a lawsuit for non-payment of costs, and she counter-sued for incompetence. There is, however, some suspicion that the relationship went beyond the professional, and that she was unhappy when his ardour cooled. There are tours from April to November; closed Mondays. *14520 River Road, T 630 552 0052, www.farnsworthhouse.org*

NOTES

SKETCHES AND MEMOS

RESOURCES

CITY GUIDE DIRECTORY

A

A10 051
1462 E 53rd Street
T 773 288 1010
www.a10hydepark.com

Aesop 056
1653 N Damen Avenue
T 872 802 4626
www.aesop.com

Alinea 044
1723 N Halsted Street
T 312 867 0110
www.alinea-restaurant.com

Andrew Rafacz 066
835 W Washington Boulevard
T 312 404 9188
www.andrewrafacz.com

Anteprima 032
5316 N Clark Street
T 733 506 9990
www.anteprimachicago.net

Aon Center 013
200 E Randolph Street

Aqua Tower 073
225 N Columbus Drive

Art Institute of Chicago 074
159 E Monroe Street
T 312 443 3600
www.artic.edu

Au Cheval 047
800 W Randolph Street
T 312 929 4580
www.auchevalchicago.com

Avec 032
615 W Randolph Street
T 312 377 2002
www.avecrestaurant.com

Aviary 032
955 W Fulton Market
T 312 226 0868
www.theaviary.com

B

Bavette's Bar & Boeuf 047
218 W Kinzie Street
T 312 624 8154
www.bavettechicago.com

Big Star 032
1531 N Damen Avenue
T 773 235 4039
www.bigstarchicago.com

Billy Sunday 051
3143 W Logan Boulevard
T 773 661 2485
www.billy-sunday.com

Blackbird 030
619 W Randolph Street
T 312 715 0708
www.blackbirdrestaurant.com

Boeufhaus 052
1012 N Western Avenue
T 773 661 2116
www.boeufhaus.com

Boleo 017
The Gray
122 W Monroe Street
T 312 750 9007
www.boleochicago.com

C

The Charleston 054
2076 N Hoyne Avenue
T 773 489 4757
www.charlestonbarchicago.com

HOTELS

ADDRESSES AND ROOM RATES

Chicago Athletic Association 020
Room rates:
double, from $250;
Founders Suite, from $1,200
12 S Michigan Avenue
T 312 940 3552
www.chicagoathletichotel.com

Four Seasons 016
Room rates:
double, from $375
120 E Delaware Place
T 312 280 8800
www.fourseasons.com/chicago

The Gray 017
Room rates:
double, from $300;
King Spa Studio, from $465
122 W Monroe Street
T 877 771 7031
www.grayhotelchicago.com

InterContinental 016
Room rates:
double, from $180
505 N Michigan Avenue
T 312 944 4100
www.icchicagohotel.com

The James 022
Room rates:
double, from $180;
Penthouse Loft, from $900
55 E Ontario Street
T 312 337 1000
www.jameshotels.com/chicago

The Langham 021
Room rates:
double, from $400;
Classic River View Suite, from $1,200
330 N Wabash Avenue
T 312 923 9988
www.chicago.langhamhotels.com

Park Hyatt 016
Room rates:
double, from $350
800 N Michigan Avenue
T 312 335 1234
chicago.park.hyatt.com

The Peninsula 016
Room rates:
double, from $500
108 E Superior Street
T 312 337 2888
chicago.peninsula.com

Radisson Blu Aqua Hotel 073
Room rates:
double, from $190
Aqua Tower
221 N Columbus Drive
T 312 565 5258
www.radissonblu.com

The Ritz-Carlton 016
Room rates:
double, from $280
Water Tower Place
160 E Pearson Street
T 312 266 1000
www.ritzcarlton.com/chicago

The Robey 018
  Room rates:
  double, from $185;
  Corner Suite, from $315
  2018 W North Avenue
  T 872 315 3050
  www.therobey.com

The Robey Hall 019
  Room rates:
  double, from $150
  2022 W North Avenue
  T 872 315 3080
  www.therobeyhall.com

Sofitel 016
  Room rates:
  double, from $140
  20 E Chestnut Street
  T 312 324 4000
  www.sofitel-chicago.com

Soho House 016
  Room rates:
  double, from $250
  113-125 N Green Street
  T 312 521 8000
  www.sohohousechicago.com

WALLPAPER* CITY GUIDES

Executive Editor
Jeremy Case

Authors
JC Gabel
Ari Bendersky
Nick Compton

Deputy Editor
Belle Place

Photography Editor
Rebecca Moldenhauer

Junior Art Editor
Jade R Arroyo

Editorial Assistant
Charlie Monaghan

Contributors
Daniëlle Siobhán Mol
Marta Bausells

Interns
Jonny Clowes
Sasha Mather

Chicago Imprint
First published 2007
Fifth edition 2017

ISBN 978 0 7148 7534 7

More City Guides
www.phaidon.com/travel

Follow us
@wallpaperguides

Contact
wcg@phaidon.com

Original Design
Loran Stosskopf
Map Illustrator
Russell Bell

Production Controller
Gif Jittiwutikarn

Wallpaper* Magazine
161 Marsh Wall
London E14 9AP
contact@wallpaper.com

Editor-in-Chief
Tony Chambers

Wallpaper*® is a
registered trademark
of Time Inc (UK)

Phaidon Press Limited
Regent's Wharf
All Saints Street
London N1 9PA

Phaidon Press Inc
65 Bleecker Street
New York, NY 10012

All prices and venue
information are correct
at time of going to press,
but are subject to change.

A CIP Catalogue record for
this book is available from
the British Library.

PHOTOGRAPHERS

William Zbaren
150 North Riverside, p011
Lake Shore Drive
apartments, p014
Smyth, p033
Honey's, p036
Estereo, p037
Income Tax, pp048-049
Boeufhaus, pp052-053
Steven Haulenbeek
(photographed in the
Spertus Institute for
Jewish Learning and
Leadership), p055
Museum of Contemporary
Art, pp060-061
Volume Gallery, p062
Art Institute of Chicago,
pp074-075
Gary Comer Youth Center,
pp078-079
John Hancock Center, p080
Lake Point Tower, p081
Mansueto Library,
pp082-083
Eleanor Boathouse at Park
571, pp086-087
Mint Home, p093
Johnson Wax Building,
p098
Farnsworth House,
pp102-103

Roger Casas
The Robey, p018, p019
Chicago Athletic
Association, p020
Duck Duck Goat, p034,
p035
Parachute, p041
Modern Times, pp094-095

Loren Fiedler
Tribune Tower, p010
Aon Center, p013
Marina City, p015
The Langham, p021
Publican Quality Meats,
p028
Parson's Chicken &
Fish, p040
Bavette's Bar &
Boeuf, p047
Green Street Smoked
Meats, p050
Billy Sunday, p051
Gallery Aesthete,
pp090-091

David Burke
Proxi, p038, p039

Doug Fogelson/DRFP
Tribune Campus, p029
Robie House, p085

**Matthew Hranek/
Art + Commerce**
Johnson Wax
Building, p099

Tim Johnson
Kavi Gupta Gallery,
pp026-027

Nathan Kirkman
North Christian Church,
p100

Mandy Lancia
Martha Mae, p089

Tom Rossiter
Logan Center for the Arts,
p084

Paul Toczynski
Chase Tower, p077

Brian Willette
Willis Tower, p012
The Peninsula Spa, p025
Wright Gallery, pp064-065
Aqua Tower, p073
Fisher Studio Houses, p076

Alamy
Cloud Gate, p067

**Panoramic Images/
Getty Images**
Chicago city view,
inside front cover
Milwaukee Art Museum,
p097

CHICAGO
A COLOUR-CODED GUIDE TO THE HOT 'HOODS

THE LOOP
Innovative builds at every turn include the world's first, and some of its finest, skyscrapers

LINCOLN PARK
Chicago's gilded youth have made this area their own, although its light is fading now

SOUTH LOOP
Capone-era warehouses loom over a renascent 'hood of bars, bookshops and eateries

NEAR NORTH
The Magnificent Mile has to be the first port of call for any self-respecting retail junkie

WEST LOOP
The meatpackers were usurped by media types as the zone gentrified into a hip hangout

GOLD COAST
Spectacular residential architecture signals the home of the Windy City's wealthiest

ANDERSONVILLE/LAKE VIEW
This amalgamation of districts includes sporty Wrigleyville and gay village Boystown

WICKER PARK/LOGAN SQUARE
Pretty townhouses and relaxed caffeine pitstops attract a cool and creative crowd

For a full description of each neighbourhood, see the Introduction.
Featured venues are colour-coded, according to the district in which they are located.

It was time to stop running....

Suddenly Ethan's hands were cradling her face, one thumb tentatively stroking the swollen bud of her lower lip. "Frannie," he whispered hoarsely, and then again, "Frannie."

"No!" She pushed herself violently from him, taking a few quick, unsteady steps backward, her eyes wide and wary.

He didn't move, and somehow Frances found that more ominous than if he had tried to overpower her. He just stood there, bright strands of blond hair quivering over his brow. His rain-soaked T-shirt clung to his chest, outlining the musculature that rose and fell rapidly with each breath.

"Excuse me," Frances breathed, in panicked, automatic politeness that was silly under the circumstances. She moved quickly to push past him, only to find herself spun around when his hand snaked out to grasp her wrist.

"You're running away from yourself, Frannie, not me."

MELINDA CROSS would love her readers to believe she was kidnapped as a child by an obscure nomadic tribe and rescued by a dashing adventurer. Actually, though, she is a wonderfully imaginative American writer who is married to a true romantic. Every spring, without fail, when the apple orchard blooms, her husband gathers a blanket, glasses and wine and leads Melinda out to enjoy the fragrant night air. Romantic fantasy? Nonsense, she says. This is the stuff of real life.

Books by Melinda Cross

Don't miss any of our special offers. Write to us at the following address for information on our newest releases.

Harlequin Reader Service
P.O. Box 1397, Buffalo, NY 14240
Canadian address: P.O. Box 603,
Fort Erie, Ont. L2A 5X3